Operation
"American Dream"

How to Overcome Battles,
Achieve Your Biggest Dreams,
and Create a Lasting Legacy

Howard S. Rixie Sr.

Operation American Dream: How to Overcome Battles, Achieve Your Biggest Dreams and Create a Lasting Legacy
Published by Quality Inventing Futures
Salcha, Alaska

ISBN: 978-0-578-29971-6
SELF-HELP / Personal Growth / Success

Cover by Nick Zellinger, copyright owned by Howard Rixie.
Interior design byVictoria Wolf, wolfdesignandmarketing.com, copyright owned by Howard Rixie.

QUANTITY PURCHASES: Schools, companies, professional groups, clubs, and other organizations may qualify for special terms when ordering quantities of this title. For information, email hsrixie@gmail.com.

"We hold these truths to be self-evident, that all men are created equal, that they are endowed by their Creator with certain unalienable Rights, that among these are Life, Liberty and the pursuit of Happiness." —*Declaration of Independence*

It's about … a young American adult accepting the American Dream is anything you want it to be, and is possible, if you have the ability, aspiration, and drive to achieve it; and willfully pursue a state of happiness defined only by you, within the liberty afforded you.

~~~~~~~~~~~~~~~~~~~~~~~~~~~~~

Chase—Even after your passing, you still inspire me to just do it!
Dodie—The rock in my very being who I am.

Contents

Preface

WHAT WAS THE IMPETUS for writing this book? Over the course of my career, I found myself encountering several adults, mostly those who, in their youth, hadn't known what they wanted out of life and now, as adults, were just wandering.

I often hear or see young people expressing a vast number of reasons for social or economic circumstances that prevent them from living a life better than they are in the present day. I see people living paycheck to paycheck, if that. I also see others who believe they are making their bid on life, with a reasonably good paying job, yet they are doing so without any real dream place or circumstance in mind; often they're just making do rather than driving toward a dream that is super special to them or their families. They survive, but endlessly wander on the fringes of their real possibilities.

I found it heartbreaking to see so many wandering with no apparent means or true desire to change their course in life and find true happiness. And I've seen this as a legacy for the generations that will follow them. In response, I developed a simple 1-page 5-year plan people could employ to guide them to a better life. I frequently used this tool to mentor those who were interested and willing, and now I want to share it with a broader audience.

With this tool, I am committed to providing an understanding of key contributors to achieving the American Dream and finding true happiness, and doing it passionately. I offer a way to look beyond the choices being made to just survive and find a pathway to living the unimaginable, ultimate American Dream. I help readers envision their personal life in retirement, the life and happiness enjoyed during that journey, and the impact of the legacy they leave behind for generations to come. Life is not simple; nor is building a legacy, nor is achieving the American Dream. This book is for those willing to make a commitment to themselves and find their American Dream.

CHAPTER I
Value Based Inspiration

WHILE THIS BOOK IS PRINCIPALLY a tool for planning an American Dream, it is even more so about the journey that includes dissecting key aspects of life, finding your inner self, and putting your plan to paper, then ultimately into action. The journey toward creating a real path to the American Dream starts with reflection; and sometimes this includes a significant emotional experience.

I know not everyone is God-fearing, but I am, and that's a personal choice. What I have learned over my life is that there is a grand plan or purpose for each of us; the old question of why was I put on this planet? Much like a sculptor looking at a new block of stone, your job is to find and uncover what's hidden inside.

Each person goes through a journey, or a discovery process toward your plan or purpose, whether knowingly or unknowingly. Along your personal journey, life (or God) sometimes challenges or even breaks you in order to refine your understanding or remind you of your purpose. These challenges range from minor impediments, or chuck holes in the road, to major catastrophic events like job loss, heartbreak, homelessness, divorce, disease, and even the death of a loved one. Each of these challenges creates an opportunity to intensify your strength, much like a blacksmith who repeatedly heats up and pounds a new knife blade with each rendition increasing its strength, durability, and sharpened edge.

Life is much like most vacations where you come home with a suitcase full of trinkets, most of which, in the end, just become needless clutter; life is the same, you accumulate clutter that adds no value to your dream. The inevitable challenges in life give us pause, a moment of reflection, and fuel a purging of baggage or impurities that blind us from imagining our dream. Think of the last time you did a deep cleaning of your room, house, or garage; once done, it feels refreshing, with thoughts of new possibilities. For each person, your personal challenge is to live a clutter-free life that fuels the possible. You constantly experience these challenges, and in each instance, you are challenged to find yourself and revisit the question of what your purpose in life is. To articulate my point, allow me to give you a characterization of what gave me the greatest drive to my dream.

I grew up in a very humble family. I can remember the big farm house. Downstairs, there was a bedroom for Mom and Dad, and another for a nearly always visiting grandpa (afflicted with Parkinson) or great grandpa (widowed). There was a large living room where many extended family gatherings took place. In the country kitchen, we found a readily apparent absence of modern amenities. The most pronounced figure just outside the reach of the stove was a large, almost barn-like door turned dinner table with long benches at its sides, where my family shared our meals and many other activities over the years. Upstairs was an open bay that looked much like an Army barracks. Along the length of both sides of the room were several army surplus metal beds, each with a 4-inch army mattress and a green wool blanket. At the foot of each bed lay a green wooden footlocker, and between each pair of beds was a small bookshelf. These very simple bed spaces provided a place for 6 growing boys to sleep, along with my dad's youngest brother, and often, another younger uncle and the other grandpa not sleeping downstairs.

I remember many different symbols of a time far removed from life as we know it today. I can recall the milkman delivering milk, eggs, and cheese. I readily recollect many times where ladies from across the community gathered downstairs with Mom, working on crafts and things, and how Dad and the rest of us were banished upstairs, entertaining each other with songs played on Dad's guitar. I can remember the neighborhood kids coming to play baseball; it was our brood of family members against the neighbors. I fondly reflect on time spent in the fields chasing rabbits and pheasants, and tending to the chicken coop for the stew pot. There were many monumental and historical moments watched on a very small black & white TV console, where we witnessed the death of President Kennedy and the landing on the moon, to name a few. I relished visits to the farms of an endless list of relatives. I felt as if I was related to nearly everyone in the community, somehow, someway.

My favorite relative was my grandmother, my mom's mom; visiting her home was amazing. While she lived a very modest life, she projected an unmatched richness. Her home was spotless, well-organized, and adorned with small tokens of affection given to her by many people, young and old, whom she had helped in their greatest time of need, no matter the price or personal sacrifice. I couldn't help but adore her as I watched her emit an angelic aura filled with love, wholesome values, very well-defined principles, and courtesy with everyone she encountered. My grandmother emphatically expected the same from my brothers and me.

Looking about at my family, it was easy for me to believe we were a living testament to the American Dream. No, we weren't rich in terms of wealth, but we were extremely wealthy in terms of family, and we shared an optimism that each of my brothers and I were going to succeed in life. Collectively, we were confident that we'd be able to get an education, find that special one, have a house with a picket fence, have a family, and a life void of hard times. Yet, my life was turned upside down and inside out in a seeming blink of an eye.

In a matter of 6 months, my grandmother was killed in an unimaginable car accident, a faulty furnace caused our family home to burn down, my mom & dad's marriage was gravely strained, and all of my brothers and I were farmed out to the homes of relatives and friends. From that moment forward, my perspective of the American Dream was shattered. I felt like the Christmas snow globe that had held our lives and dreams in an animated state, for all to observe, was smashed to the ground and shattered into a million pieces.

In what seemed another blink, in a matter of a few months, I experienced the greatest slap in the face in terms of my beliefs. My father found another companion and became absent from my life. While farming us brothers out to family and friends was supposed to be a temporary measure, my two older brothers had become what today we call "couch surfers" and disconnected from the rest of us, which became a permanent part of our up-bringing. At the same time, I witnessed my mom struggle with decisions regarding the care for one of my brothers who was mentally challenged, who eventually was removed from our daily lives and became a resident in a special home. And lastly, I witnessed my mom work tirelessly at three jobs to house and feed my two remaining brothers and me. Our family unit had become shattered into a state of total despair.

While my mom could barely feed and clothe us, I can recall Mom sharing a belief passed down from my grandmother, that no matter what, make sure the kids have a Christmas; and that she did every year. No, it wasn't the latest and greatest of anything, but it included several little gifts that fostered that special feeling of Christmas celebration and thankfulness. The other moment that carved its way into my perspective was when my mom's three jobs were just not enough, and for a very short period of time, our family had to rely on public assistance and food stamps. Often, I did the shopping while Mom worked. On those occasions, I was repeatedly humiliated, at least from my perspective, each time I stood at the grocery paying the cashier with these excessively obvious forms of special money for the poor. I could feel the glare of my friends and even those who didn't know me, as if they were whispering, "Look, there's one of those lazy charity cases, unwilling to do for themselves, and living off the public dole."

These scars carved deeply into my value system for life. I pledged to myself that when I was grown, I would do everything in my power to never again experience the despair I had felt. I didn't want to just dream the so-called American Dream; I wanted to be the epitome of having it.

While I could spend several pages describing an endless list of events and decisions that challenged me over the other 40 years of life, I can assure you what I've described so far were, and remain, the cornerstones to what I value and base every life choice on. With that said, I will share the gravest experience I've ever had, the death of my son, Chase.

A certified boy genius, Chase had to be the best at everything he took on. He was a cross-country ski medalist at the Arctic Winter games. He graduated from high school and started college when he was just 16 years old. He was an avid weightlifter. He completed a bachelor's degree in electrical engineering and a master's degree in electronic communications before his 22nd birthday. In partnership with the love of his life and wife, Sarah, by his 30th birthday he had achieved success by every meaning of the word; he was the top 1% in his peer group. With all that Chase was able to achieve, he struggled with three major issues or demons; what more could he offer this world, how could he be the best at whatever that was; and why should he put forth the effort, given the feckless direction society and the world were evolving toward? In the end, Chase's demons won.

Chase watched Me mentor young people throughout his life, and if he was still with us, he would chastise me if I wasn't sharing what I have to offer the generations to come. He'd say, "Buck it up, Dad, and get it done!"

Yes, I take great pause and reflection on how life's events shape who we are forever more. In homage to my son, I'd like you to join me, and walk through the footsteps of a young man I'm calling Buck as he tries to search for, find, and experience his version of Life, Liberty, and Pursuit of Happiness. While Buck is a fictious character, his circumstance in life is predicated on the boy next door, growing up in a family with very modest means, living in a heavily populated community, and exposed to the challenges found in any city. The remainder of this book is about Buck's journey to finding his American Dream.

In starting your own journey, I hope you enjoy the trek, and not only find your inner self, but your true purpose in life; knowing both will play a critical role in fueling your American Dream.

CHAPTER II

Your Legacy Imagined

APPROACHING ANY PROJECT with the end in mind is always important. Ask yourself what's it going to look like? So, before approaching the present, let's take a moment to imagine how your American Dream might materialize in your final stage in life.

I've always been a zealot when it came to history. I am infatuated with the pioneer life. I always believed I should have grown up in another era, like the 1880s-1900s. One of my fascinations has always been the lifestyles of Native Americans. An example was their use of sweat lodges. Sweat lodges were used for many purposes, but mostly for ceremonies. The Pluralism Project at Harvard University writes,

"The ceremonies of the sweat lodge include rites of preparation, prayer, and purification. Today, the sweat lodge plays a very significant role in the lives of Native communities in their efforts to bring about personal and social healing and commitment to collective values. The sweat lodge is a structure charged with sacred meaning and power. Participants experience a purification of body, mind,

7

spirit, and community as they feel the heat of the steam and offer their prayers and songs. Because one enters the sweat lodge naked and undergoes a rite of cleansing and commitment, the sweat lodge rituals are said to be a kind of rebirth. Perhaps because this purification integrates physical, psychological, social, and spiritual well-being, the sweat lodge has become central in contemporary Native American rites and practices of healing."[1]

Ikce Wicasa, SWEAT-LODGE (INIPI)

This practice has represented pure intrigue for me. I can only imagine what they really experienced in that setting. The thought of the elders, family, and friends being directly part of and sharing the process is fascinating. What a way to elicit complete understanding by those closest to you?

I wanted Buck to use the same amount of vigor and commitment to help imagine and define his American Dream. I asked him to imagine a grand celebration far in the future, where a large group of his family and friends had gathered to celebrate his 100th birthday. Those gathered put together a holograph video presentation to depict the chronology of his life experiences.

Segments were dedicated to his achievements and moments of joy, and the bond he nurtured among family and friends, how he capitalized on educational opportunities, how his career evolved, how he amassed his material wealth; how he gained financial independence, and how it transcended into unimaginable generosity, and lastly, how spirituality played a role in the way he discovered and practiced life's truths. As Buck envisioned this celebration, he could only imagine how that moment would be charged with emotions of gratitude, achievement, and joy. He experienced a wow moment, the first of many to come!

I reminded Buck life is not perfect. Life is made up of many decisions that choreograph your path in life, and the outcomes of those decisions color the landscape of your journey. At 100 years old, knowing what he would likely know then, such a celebration and moment of reflection would likely stir up several events or decisions he wished he could have changed.

Let's be real! Buck has only lived less than one quarter of such a lifetime, and doesn't have the knowledge, experience, and true comprehension of the changes that are integral to the later stages of life. Things like: the birth of a child, promotion at a job, buying a first home, a child's graduation or marriage, the joy of a newborn grandchild, paying off a mortgage, retiring from a life-long career, the death of a loved one or the absence of life-long friends within his daily circle. etc.

To bring Buck's hopes and dreams to life, I had him try to imagine what he would see and experience in his sweat lodge ceremony. He spent endless hours, over several days, just trying find every corner of his dream and truths.

As Buck began sharing his thoughts with me, I explained the concept of a dream board, or vision board, is a collage of images, pictures, and affirmations of one's dreams and desires, designed to serve as a source of inspiration and motivation.[2] After hearing about this concept, Buck just couldn't comprehend how a bunch of pictures could help bring his dream to reality. I explained completing a vision board helps articulate the dream; as the saying goes, a picture is worth a thousand words. I also rhetorically asked Buck, "How do you eat an elephant?" And then I answered, "One bite at a time." Just like the first bite of an elephant, the first step to a dream is important. In Buck's case, he had no destination in mind, nor a map to any destination, nor a plan he'd use to make the journey.

Exercise - Make a preliminary vision board.

I gave Buck the following exercise. I told him nowadays we are bombarded with imagery over the internet, so building a vision board is extremely easy in the craft sense, but it requires an immense amount of unconstrained thought and imagination.

The task was comprised of these steps:

1. Grab internet images - capture all those things you want to do, see, have, be, love, feel, etc.
2. Choose your images — if it grabs your attention, it has struck a nerve, for good or bad.
3. Think back to that 100-year celebration and moments of reflection — did you miss anything?
4. Create a collage of your images — just get them on paper (electronically).
5. Find a temporary home for your collage — maybe on your desktop.

Buck had spent the better part of a week on completing this exercise and was overwhelmed with how much information could be captured using this method. I congratulated him with great excitement. He had created his first success in a long journey — his American Dream was one step closer.

CHAPTER III
The Journey Continues — Destination Wayward

ON HIS VISION BOARD, Buck had captured everything imaginable about the kind of life he wanted to live, and both of us were feeling stupendous. He was feeling proud and accomplished. I reminded him life is much like a chess game, and for every game there needs to be a strategy. Life isn't just a case of going to college, finding love, getting married, having kids, and becoming a millionaire. I pointed out that, while his vision board had captured his destination and some of the scenery he was likely to see along the way, he still lacked a road map for how he was going to get there. Buck was beginning to realize how completing his journey was going to be much more complex than he first thought. He was becoming frustrated.

Buck knew his dream was going to take several years, but he didn't understand why he needed to create a detailed road map. I explained it was like planning a long road trip across the country; a typical road map might be able to show you many likely travel routes, but what about the unexpected? How is that map going to account for an unexpected flat tire, or running out of gas, or the absence of a hotel, construction detours, bad weather, etc.? I asked Buck, "What's your plan for the unexpected?" By now, he was really conflicted and he asked why he couldn't just deal with them as they occur?

I asked him what was the shortest distance between two points? He correctly responded, a straight line. I convinced him our goal is to find the straight line and minimize the impact of any deviations or delays on the trip. In a lengthy discussion, the two of us threw out a number of possible interruptions and dissected how their impacts could not only change the trajectory in the short or long term, but also how they could become complete barriers to getting to that dream destination, and force him to accept a Plan B destination — one that might not be anything close to his original dream, forcing him to settle for something far short of the original dream. I asked Buck if he was willing to just settle, and he emphatically replied no!

To be successful on this front, Buck needed to become cognizant of the landscape around him and how it could possibly impact the path to his dream. We had a lengthy discussion, and part of that discussion addressed the following questions:

1. Who's or what's in Buck's circle of influence?

To answer this question, I instructed Buck to look around his circle of friends and neighbors, and try to make a list identifying the good, the bad, and the ugly. I assured him that he'd be able to quickly identify the "Oh Yeah!" and the "Heck No!" people in his circle.

I also cautioned Buck to not overlook those people who are not so much in-your-face obvious people of influence. He quickly thought of an example, a neighborhood man he admired, who he often saw stopping whatever he was doing at the drop of a dime, no matter what was going on, to lend a helping hand to neighborhood kids. I said, "Yes, this was a prime example of someone doing something seemingly invisible, yet being very impactful in defining the kind of man you might want to become."

Buck was able to rattle off a list of people in his circle, good and bad, and how they could play a significant role in helping him achieve his dream. He was also able to identify a number of resources he might be able to capitalize on.

Another key component to Buck becoming more self-aware of his circumstances was the following question:

2. What are the key stops and barriers you are likely to encounter along the way to achieving your dream?

What are the milestones you would really like to experience or achieve? What things fall short or are totally unacceptable, and where are the lines or barriers you're willing to breach, or not? Like with the previous question, Buck was able to rattle off a number of issues, milestones, and likely barriers. While I applauded Buck for his command of his surroundings, I reminded him that until they are actionable, they are just a hodge-podge of loose thoughts. He needed to tie them all together by putting them on paper, with a timeline and check points. Then, and only then, would he have an action-able road map.

To offer a solution, I introduced Buck to a very simple tool, my 1-page 5-year plan. I used this example to demonstrate how he could consolidate all those loose thoughts and aspirations onto one page.

T. Jefferson - American Dream Road Map   As of date: 1976

	Currently	Less Than 1 Year	1 – 3 Years	3 – 5 Years	5 Years	American Dream End-Sate
Materially	Live with Parents	Buy a Get-By Car with Cash / Move out of Parents / Share home with friends	Maintain Get-By Car / Renting own home / Used-a-Bit Furnishings	Buy long term car w/ cash / Renting own home / Get/Have compliment of furnishings	Maintain long term car / Buy a home with 25% down payment	Own home outright / Furnished comfortably / Replace car with cash at-will / Own vacation home
Financially	College debt / Small credit card debt	Living Debt Free / $1000 emergency fund	3-month emergency fund	6-month emergency fund / Saved a fully funded down payment for house	Putting 15% of income toward 401K fund	Giving 10% of gross income toward charity / 401K greater than $1M
Employment	College Student	Entry level professional job	Named a Lead over a team / Have network of associates	Named a Project Manager / Built a network of expert	Named a mid-level manager	Retired by 50 years old
Education	Enrolled in Electrical Engineering B.S.	Start a Masters degree in Electrical Engineering	Graduate w/ Masters in Electrical Engineering / Completed some leadership training	Receive Professional Engineer Certificate / Completed some management training	Completing Continuing Education training requirements	Studying Philanthropy
Family	Single with core friends	Casual dating	Nurturing a long term relationship	Serious long term relationship	Married – maybe	Celebrating 25+ years of marriage / Enjoying children and grandkids
Spiritually	Positive – faith	Dabbling in community service projects / Defining commitment to faith-based activities	Active volunteer in community service projects / Have a few pet rock interests / Involved in some faith-based activities	Lead – Annual community service project / Involved in faith-based activities	Up and coming community civic leader / Possibly leading a faith-based activity	Active community civic leader / Leading a pet rock project / Possibly leading a faith-based activity

I suggested to Buck that, if he's to achieve his American Dream, he needs to have all of the data related to that dream in mind when walking through the process of developing his first, yes, his first, 5-Year Plan. I assured him building this plan would make all the difference in achieving his American Dream and not having to settle for anything less.

Buck's first glance at this tool prompted an, "Oh, I got this." I quickly reminded him the most significant part of this tool was not the tool itself, but rather the journey he'd take in developing the plan, one module at a time. The journey would frame and put into context the What, When, Where, Why, and How. I implored Buck to not cheat himself of the journey! To do otherwise would only open the door to and fuel the unexpected and delays along his trip, or even change the final destination. Buck embraced the opportunity to make this journey with me.

CHAPTER IV

The American Dream

NOW THAT BUCK HAD ACCUMULATED a massive amount of imagery that attested to his wants, desires, passions, and lines he was not willing to cross, that seemingly summed up his thinking, he was fully charged and ready to lay it all out.

Buck and I were fortunate to be taking an excursion to the port of Valdez, Alaska, nearly 400 miles from our homes in North Pole. We were fired up about the opportunity to catch some fish, halibut specifically. We talked of catching "the big one" and maybe even winning the fishing derby prize money. We even teased each other about who was going to catch the first fish, and the biggest. We knew the record was over 300 pounds. Buck said he was going to set a new record. I laughed and said, "That sounds like a pipe dream." I took advantage of the conversation to talk about Buck's American Dream.

I challenged him on whether he understood the concept of the American Dream? I asked this question because I wanted him to truly appreciate how young Americans, more often than not, constrain their dreams rather than embracing the opportunities set within the American Dream.

Buck wasn't sure if what he thought to be his dream was really an American Dream. He confessed he wanted to go into this journey with his eyes wide open, and he wanted to fully understand what was the American Dream and what might influence achieving it. During our 6-hour road trip, Buck and I discussed what is the American Dream and how it has evolved. We discussed the following:

In our nation's beginning, this country was the new world, a land being explored for all its new-found bounties. With all the bewilderment surrounding what this vast territory had to offer, many early settlers migrated here to change their course in life. Many immigrated here to be free of oppressive governments that impeded their way of life, whether it was their ability to practice their religion, the absence of representation in their government, excessive taxes, governmental over-regulation, agricultural plight, class warfare, suppression of the opportunity to advance their position in society, etc. Immigrants were looking for a new beginning; and they did so with great vigor.

The trek of the migrants was not easy and not without grave personal sacrifice, including, in many cases, tragic losses of life within their family circles. For those who embraced a strong work ethic and zealous drive for change, their migration offered them what they had hoped, opening the door to a new life, and answered most, if not all of their original reasons or motivations to migrate. The sacrifices made by these pioneers shaped a new culture of social norms.

After more than a century in the new world, the various nations influencing the settlement of America found themselves extracting the cream of all the new-found riches. These nations reaped the benefit of the riches with total disregard for those exploring, finding, harvesting, and bringing them to market. Societal norms developed much like the evolution of a drug addict; getting enticed by a new-found pleasure drug, seeking a repeat of that pleasure over and over again, and eventually doing so with total disregard to the methods, means, and impact of achieving that pleasure. In this case, the drug of choice included the spoils and riches from the new world. These very practices and disregard became the prevailing impetus for the American revolution. The founding fathers from every colony rose up in unity to eventually declare independence and codify the union with the ratification and implementation of the U.S. Constitution.

While the founding fathers wanted all grievances by their constituents to be addressed in crafting both the *Declaration of Independence* and the *U.S. Constitution*, they didn't do it blindly. They wanted both documents and their outcomes to be enduring. To that end, they contrasted the successes and failures of many nations and their forms of governance, and used a value system of social norms grounded in a faith of a Creator as a guide.

The founding fathers paved the way for each of us to find happiness when they published the *Declaration of Independence*. Unfortunately, few have actually read the document so central to American citizenship; and for others, their understanding of its substance has waned in the 21st century.

[The text of Declaration of Independence is offered in an annex to this book. Set aside a moment to read this founding document, if not as a reminder, then to foster a common point of perspective.]

Early colonists were fed up with life as it was in their home lands, chose change, and immigrated to the new world. When those same forces of power and influence began to permeate and infest their lives again, they threw complacency and complicity aside, and became a formidable active citizenry in defining a new social norm, purpose, and protection from tyranny.

The founders did not leave achieving their charter of independence to happenstance — they plotted a path to bring it into reality by crafting and publishing the *U.S. Constitution*; the preamble of which reads:

We the People of the United States, in Order to form a more perfect Union, establish Justice, insure domestic Tranquility, provide for the common defense, promote the general Welfare, and secure the

Blessings of Liberty to ourselves and our Posterity, do ordain and establish this Constitution for the United States of America.

In both the *Declaration of Independence* and the *U.S. Constitution,* the cornerstone belief is that all people are born with an unalienable right to freedom.

Declaration of Independence: "We hold these truths to be self-evident, that all men are created equal, that they are endowed by their Creator with certain unalienable Rights, that among these are Life, Liberty and the pursuit of Happiness."

So, what does the term "unalienable" mean? *Dictionary.com* defines it as, "not transferable to another or not capable of being taken away or denied." The *Declaration of Independence* stipulated each of us, as members of mankind, have unalienable rights that no one can take away, nor can they be transferred to someone else. It further stipulated that some of these rights include "life, liberty and the pursuit of happiness."

What did the founding fathers mean by life, liberty and the pursuit of happiness? In their simplest form

- A person shall not be deprived of their *life*;
- A person should have the *liberty* to live as they please;
- A person shall be free to pursue their individual *happiness*, as they envision it.

These rights are constrained in so much as one person's exercise of their rights cannot infringe on another's exercise of their rights; and the laws we collectively make have that primary purpose of defining the lines of infringement.

The life blood of the founders' declaration, that "Life, Liberty and the pursuit of Happiness" were unalienable rights, endowed by our Creator, stipulated every man or woman has these rights, and no other person may deprive them of the same. Furthermore, it also requires us to acknowledge the existence of a being, entity, or deity greater than mankind, while the latter does not mean a non-believer does not have these rights. But it does infer the depth and scope of these rights are value—and moral-based, and our society governs or polices itself by finding the balance between infringement of citizens and those values.

Amidst our discussion, Buck was trying to relate it to his dream. He finally got frustrated and blurted out, "What does this have to do with the American Dream?" I responded that in making these documents, our founders fostered or codified an environment where each citizen would have the freedom to live **life** to the fullest, reaping the blessings of **liberty**, in the pursuit of their own self-defined **happiness** as they would have it; and every American could broach these aspirations without being impeded by the government. I pointed out that several of the founders also wrote in many forums that achieving happiness is not guaranteed; rather, it requires a passion to seek it out and the drive to endure the sacrifices necessary to achieve it.

We both concluded that, rather than constraining Americans with limits or boundaries, the founders advocated for a seemingly limitless American dreams. Happiness was boundless, limited only by one's imagination. We then discussed how to define or describe the American Dream. In a quick internet search, we found an article titled *The American Dream* by Adam Barone on investopedia.com.

"The American dream is the belief that anyone, regardless of where they were born or what class they were born into, can attain their own version of success in a society in which upward mobility is possible for everyone. The American dream is believed to be achieved through sacrifice, risk-taking, and hard work, rather than by chance."

KEY TAKEAWAYS

- The term "American Dream" was coined in a best-selling book in 1931 titled *Epic of America*, by James Truslow Adams, who described it as "that dream of a land in which life should be better and richer and fuller for everyone, with opportunity for each according to ability or achievement."
- The American Dream was aided by a number of factors that gave the United States a competitive advantage over other countries.
- Homeownership and education are often seen as paths to achieving the American Dream.
- Though the definition of the American Dream has changed to mean different things to different generations, it's undoubtedly part of the American ethos, and likely always will.[3]

We discussed how many people would argue that happiness is found by becoming rich; being a millionaire or billionaire eliminates any wanting, thus making you happy. Yet others believe the richest man could be found among the poorest, because their happiness was found in enjoying the richness in life. We agreed that without question, the American Dream has changed over the years, and so have the sacrifices typically taken to achieve it. I stressed that the colonial beginning of the American Dream was found in the opportunity to leave an oppressive country and come to America to find freedom to practice religious beliefs, own land, and share in the richness of a new world. In the early twentieth century the American Dream transformed into a stereotype of marriage, family, owning a home with a picket fence, etc.

I went on to surmise having endured a revolution, civil war, two world wars. and a depression, achieving the American Dream was grounded in a number of contributors: becoming educated, caring for and feeding each other, building a reputation for a strong work ethic, developing a pay-as-you-go financing system, making choices based on values, fostering honor among individuals as well as within the community where you lived, where a man's name or handshake was his bond, to name a few.

One of our prevailing conclusions was that a commonality in chasing the American Dream, no matter the era, was the desire by each generation to enable their offspring to have a better life than they had, with more doors open to reaping more of the American bounty and less propensity to experience hardship, despair, and deprivation of their aspirations. After sharing this experience, I could tell Buck got it — the American Dream is anything you want it to be, and is possible if you have the ability and aspiration and drive to achieve it.

CHAPTER V
A Reflection of Contributors

EVERYTHING HAD SUNK IN FOR BUCK. As he was attempting to corral his thoughts and inclinations, and squeeze them into his first draft of his 1-page plan, he had a revelation.

Buck had realized the journey for building his plan was far more involved than he originally thought. While doodling snippets into each branch of his 5-year plan may fill the boxes, he felt it was like drawing a treasure map on a bar napkin. Some things were obscure, blurred, and even absent. It was like looking at a dashboard on his car and all the instruments were inoperative; the only thing you could tell was that the engine was on. He realized he couldn't approach something so key to his dream merely by sprinkling some thoughts on paper like a soon-to-be overdue book report.

Buck and I had discussed at length the real degree of commitment it would take to put substantive meaning into his plan. He had to decide whether he was willing to commit to such an effort. With my vast number of years in the military, I suggested to Buck his plan deserved the effort and study that any General would give a war plan; lives were at stake, namely Buck's and anyone in his circle of family and friends. After a full day of reflection, Buck fully committed to making something that was harmonious with his aspirations — he wasn't willing to settle!

Buck had become committed to researching each of the following, as if each was its own battle campaign and an integral part of the overall war plan. Together, we had some creative juices and dubbed these campaigns as:

- Battle 1: **Operation Bank That** — (Financial independence),
- Battle 2: **Operation My Stuff** — (Accumulation of Material Belongings),
- Battle 3: **Operation DIY** — (Education — Tooling a path),
- Battle 4: **Operation Lunchbox** — (Building a Career — Employment),
- Battle 5: **Operation Squeeze Me** — (Bonds of Relationship — shared),
- Battle 6: **Operation Care-Bear** — (Spiritually -- Solace in practicing life truths).

CHAPTER V-A
Operation Bank That

WHILE BUCK IS A YOUNGER AMERICAN, he was not naïve when it came to the connection of wealth to anyone's dreams. Like many others, he believed if he had bottomless bags of money, how could he not be happy? The belief of not having enough money was the root of all despair experienced in the daily grind of life.

Buck had heard it all from his circle of friends. Their beliefs were founded in every daily decision making; just to name a few:

- I can't buy, a house, a car, nice clothes, because I'm poor and have no credit.
- I can't go to college because I can't afford it and can't get a scholarship.
- I can't move to where the good jobs are because I live paycheck to pay check.
- I can't change jobs because I need the health insurance I have.

Buck's thoughts on this issue were evolving. He had repeatedly heard from many sources that financial independence can be achieved by nearly anyone willing to vigorously attack that desire, but he struggled to fully understand the validity of those claims. He knew in today's era we are conditioned to live by way of debt; credit is the pathway to getting what you want or need. The success of financial institutions depends on money being moved. Those institutions are like the drug dealer on the corner. They want you hooked, and once you're hooked, you're seemingly hooked for life.

Among Buck's friends there were endless testimonies of high school kids, and even a couple of their pets, receiving unsolicited credit cards in the mail; that's the bait. Among those taking the bait, more often than not, the recipient is wowed and excited they received their very first credit card and access to a credit line of $300; it was a milestone toward becoming an adult.

They tried to be responsible by holding onto it just for an emergency. Inevitably, what was considered an out of the blue emergency of some sort happened, again and again; and soon the $300 is tapped out. At that moment, their financial independence was leveraged by an obligation to pay it off, or at least a little bit each month. Each time credit of any sort, credit card, car loan, student loan, mortgage, etc., is used, the debtor's take home pay was further leveraged by that obligation to pay. Then when those bills were compounded with the debtor's basic needs of shelter, food, clothing, transportation, medical, etc., eventually every bit of his or her income was even further leveraged. Once somebody gets in that predicament, there's seemingly no room to maneuver their finances and every unexpected expense becomes an emergency.

To makes things worse, an occasional missed or late payment becomes a repeated course of events, so now the person's credit rating is reduced, indicating to those drug dealers (financial institutions) they are now a credit risk and over extended. So, the person is now being punished for using credit, backing them into a corner with even fewer opportunities for finding relief.

Having watched family members and friends go down this path of being subservient to the credit drug dealer, Buck was convinced to find an alternative. One day he was stuck in traffic and the Dave Ramsey radio show came on. Dave and his guests were speaking about everything Buck had been thinking.

Dave Ramsey is a seven-time #1 national bestselling author, personal finance expert and host of The Ramsey Show, heard by 18 million listeners every week. He has appeared on Good Morning America, CBS This Morning, Today, Fox News, CNN, Fox Business and many more. Since 1992, Dave has helped people take control of their money, build wealth and enhance their lives. He also serves as CEO for the company Ramsey Solutions.[4]

For several days, Buck binge-listened to several of Dave Ramsey's podcasts, and he came to believe the idea of financial independence starts with living debt free — that's right, debt free!

Buck had endorsed Dave Ramsey's approach to financial independence, an approach outlined in an article published on Ramsey's website titled *What are the 7 Baby Steps*?

What are the 7 Baby Steps?

This is the plan that will help you take control of your money! Millions have followed the 7 Baby Steps and left their money worries behind. These steps lead you out of debt, help you stop living paycheck to paycheck, and give you a secure future. Here's a brief breakdown:

- Baby Step 1 — Save $1,000 for your starter emergency fund.
- Baby Step 2 — Pay off all debt (except the house) using the debt snowball.
- Baby Step 3 — Save 3—6 months of expenses in a fully funded emergency fund.

- Baby Step 4 — Invest 15% of your household income in retirement.
- Baby Step 5 — Save for your children's college fund.
- Baby Step 6 — Pay off your home early.
- Baby Step 7 — Build wealth and give.[5]

Always a skeptic, Buck found an article by Mike Capuzzo, a New York Times-bestselling author, titled *The Truth About Dave Ramsey's Baby Steps* that helped him embrace the concepts with his eyes wide open. While these steps were simple enough to understand on the surface, Buck knew it was easier said than done. But he had become a zealot. He urged all of his friends to at least check out the Dave Ramsey web site and review the material there or listen to the podcasts.

As Buck understood it, the secrets to the success many people have had using these steps were anchored in:

1. Building small successes;
2. Building and living by a budget, giving each dollar of income a stated purpose;
3. Attacking the steps with vigorous commitment.

Buck frequently shared an example of small successes with his friends. In his example, you have 10 credit type bills, and you dedicate every extra dollar toward paying off the one with the smallest balance, and you finally pay it off; a success! He acknowledges, yes, it would likely be somewhat painful, but it would give him more breathing room to attack the next lowest balance debt on the list. The wow feeling will become louder and prouder with every new success — until he would eventually be debt free!

He had also embraced the idea of a budget. In a nutshell the first step in building a budget is to list all income and expenses. By at least approximating these figures, giving every dollar a deliberate purpose begins with knowing what you're currently spending every dollar on. During this exercise, it was very illuminating to Buck. He looked back over a year at what he spent in each category of expenses, i.e., he spent $1,000 on vehicle maintenance, or on average, $19 per week. His OMG moment was when he realized he spent $300 a month on coffees and another $400 a month eating out at restaurants. Just by doing this, Buck quickly found things to do without, freeing up dollars to pay down debt. Buck had found Dave Ramsey's app called *EveryDollar*[6] to help him complete his budget process. The Ramsey method also asked him to build up an emergency fund; initially $1,000. The key component to the budgeting process was the inclusion of planning for the inevitable, i.e., replacing tires on your car is something you can forecast or anticipate, and should budget for under vehicle maintenance; that means it's no longer an emergency. In contrast, your water pipes freezing during a winter power outage is something unforeseen; that's an emergency, but you're able to reach into that emergency fund to deal with the crisis. This practice allows you to continually refine the definition of emergencies and how much you have set aside to respond to them. Everything is subject to wear and breakage. One day there will be no emergencies, but rather a planned response to an inevitable event.

Seeing the financial struggles of friends, Buck wholeheartedly recognized the need for vigorous commitment. Getting to the point where you are able to live debt free requires you to become debt free first, while simultaneously leveraging future financial decisions. Eliminating your debt requires commitment, strong commitment! It requires you to not view this as a diet where you're cutting back on certain foods (or debt). Such an approach is very likely to bring you full circle and back to your old habits, i.e., you get a consolidation loan to pay off your credit cards and reduce your payments, but never cut up and cancel the credit cards, and eventually you use them again. You haven't achieved anything; you just added another drug dealer to your portfolio.

While Buck's debt was not as extreme as his friends, he reflected back on the credit card he paid off. The sensation he got from that achievement was extremely stimulating; it was a feeling of accomplishment. Buck described it as a feeling you want again, and again. You become willing to do whatever it takes to repeat that experience, and after several of those experiences you become extremely compulsive. In essence, your new drug of choice is paying off another debt.

Using the *gazelle intensity*[7] Ramsey often advocates for, you become willing to eat a beans and rice diet, sell off unused household items, trade that $50K car (& loan) on a car fully paid for, or take another job in order to find more dollars to pay those bills off. Buck fully appreciated how employing such an intensity only accelerates the once inconceivable, elimination of debt.

Given Buck's appreciation for this process and the impact it has on life decisions and previously unthinkable new possibilities, he became committed to helping his friends find their own campaigns to financial independence. In Buck's campaign to help his friends, given the chance, he would walk them through a very simple exercise:

Exercise

1. Build a balance sheet:
   a. **Assets:** What you have or own (bank checking/savings account balances, house, car, other property, etc.).
   b. **Liabilities:** What/whom do you owe money.
   c. **Net worth:** Subtract Liabilities from Assets (a-b = Net worth).
2. Build a monthly budget — give every dollar a purpose (no slush fund dollars).
3. Answer these questions:
   a. How much debt do you want to have in: 1 year? $_____; 3 years? $ _____; 5 years? $ _____
   b. How much of an emergency fund will you have: Now? $_____ in 1 year? $_____ in 3 years? $ _____ and in 5 years? $ _____

Ironically, this very information is what Buck needed for his American Dream plan. So, after completing this exercise for himself, he was one more step closer to the American Dream he was envisioning. A loud congratulatory high five was given. The battle plan OPERATION BANK THAT was ready to go!

CHAPTER V-B
Operation My Stuff

FOR BUCK AND HIS FRIENDS TO EQUATE to how much and what they own as a measure of success was natural; it's something they can see and touch. And for those around them, they too can see it, and their response becomes a form of affirmation for the beholder, e.g., Wow! You drive a Cadillac! It's a clear path to keeping up with the Joneses. Given his desire to live debt free, Buck wanted to tame this compulsion on his journey. Here's what he learned when he dissected this dream contributor.

Most people would say their most important assets are their own homes, cars and electronics (phone, flat screen TV, etc.). Logic dictates that what we own is predicated on what we can afford. The financial practices of today have opened up a gateway to getting all those material items that seemingly make up the American Dream, and getting them early on in adulthood, without any significant sacrifice upfront. Want it now, get it now.

Many of us reflect on what we did or didn't have when we were growing up. Most of that reflection is on what we didn't have and the hardships that came with the circumstance. It also plays on our perspective about what our position or station in life is, i.e., we had to live in a government subsidized housing complex and were among the poorest of the poor. That notion compels us to change that circumstance, thus the impetus for the American Dream.

Buck needed to assess his material wealth as it stood in the present day. He had already itemized the big-ticket items on his balance sheet, but he had likely overlooked the less obvious, i.e., clothing, household furnishings, collections of any sort, etc. Making this assessment helped him define how and what he placed value on. Before addressing this task or exercise on material accumulation, I wanted to give Buck a better perspective on our collective past and get him to appreciate how our needs have become overshadowed by our wants. I shared the following thoughts:

- Our homes have gone from 300 sq ft, 1 room cabins, or extremely small farmhouses with multiple generations sharing them to 1200 sq ft post WWII single family homes, to massive 2,000-3,000 sq ft homes where everyone has a private bedroom, multiple bathrooms, two-car garages, and all of the technology you can imagine. Our homes have come a long way. But so has our debt load.
- We've gone from a period where young married couples lived with their parents until, after several years of saving, they would venture out on their own to now where graduating from high school (or not) meant freedom from all those parental restrictions to being voluntarily thrust onto the economy. With little self-control, the adage of keeping up with the Joneses has permeated through every facet of life; and the Want it now-Get it now beast grows at a feverous rate.

Yes, in today's circumstances, the American Dream is grounded in a world of materialism, and likely by way of credit. Recent generations are willing to accrue massive loads of debt so they might have what they didn't have growing up, and having it now. And why not, if banks are willing to give us credit cards? They obviously think we can afford it. In contrast, previous generations used credit, if they could get it, as a last resort, even if that meant personal sacrifice, doing without, or a perception of being poor or poorer than their neighbors.

"Until the 1920s, Americans had to save their money to buy expensive goods. However, stores developed a way for people to make expensive purchases without having to save their money first. This was called consumer credit."[8] "The 1920s was a decade of increasing conveniences for the middle class. New products made household chores easier and led to more leisure time. Products previously too expensive became affordable. New forms of financing allowed every family to spend beyond their current means. Advertising capitalized on people's hopes and fears to sell more and more goods."[9]

Consumer debt has become a way of life in the present day. In late 2017, Ramsey Solutions conducted a study of more than 1,000 U.S. adults to gain understanding of personal finance behaviors and attitudes, including the level of debt across generations and income levels. While America is listed among the world's richest nations, the average American debt continues to weigh its citizens down. Almost three out of four Americans (72%) say they are burdened by debt, including mortgages. And two-thirds of Americans (66%) reported consumer debt, with an average of $34,055 debt load per person.[10]

According to the Census Bureau's report *Income and Poverty in the United States: 2020*, "Median household income was $67,521 in 2020."[11] Furthermore, "the average American holds $53,897 in personal debt, much of it tied up in mortgages. If mortgages are excluded, the average debt would drop to $16,720."[12]

So, where have we come over the last 100 years? To answer that, we found "… the average household income in the United States in 1920 was approximately $3,269.40—that's about $42,142.08 today, with inflation;" and the average household debt was 4.2% which included the home mortgage.[13]

Contrasting the 1920 debt level to the present day, today we see an average mortgage debt of $37,177 or 55% of the average income: and non-mortgage debt of $16,720 or 24.7% of income. Combining the two measures means American spend more than 79.8% of their income on consumer debt. Either measure is far greater than the 4% of the 1920s; and so is the stress of making those payments.

Having found these facts, Buck reflected on the significant despair his grandparents and most Americans experienced during the Great Depression. He thought if that's what the impact on people's lives was with an average debt load of 4%; what would it be like with a 79% debt load?

Buck was overwhelmed! This realization was a major red flare moment in his thought process. He became all the more committed to financial independence by avoiding the ills of the "want it now, get it now" mentality. He agreed that if he wanted to make a significant contribution to achieving his American Dream, he needed to frame every purchase decision as a value-based decision. I suggested to Buck to frame those decisions around these core questions:

- Is it a want or a need?
- How does this purchase and/or use of credit impact furthering my dream?
- Does it put my dream at risk?

Those are great questions and aspirations, but again, living by them is easier said than done. True to form for his generation, Buck used his internet search engine to research the question of how best to determine a want versus a need. He found Maslow's theory, while it seemed a complex answer to his question, the simplicity of the diagram intrigued him and drew him in. In our discussion he learned, "Maslow's hierarchy of needs is a theory by Abraham Maslow, which puts forward that people are motivated by five basic categories of needs: physiological, safety, love, esteem, and self-actualization."[14]

In essence, Maslow thought it was human nature to be motivated to address lower-level needs before attempting to address the higher-levels, e.g., you need to satisfy your need for food and shelter before thinking of finding a soulmate. He also thought that while satisfying the lower-level needs first is core to our existence, it doesn't prevent us from attempting to satisfy higher level needs before they truly become immediate needs. Decisions or actions taken to act on these choices do, however, put the lower levels at risk.

In discussing this with Buck, I offered the following example: You buy a large house that far exceeds your needs, and maybe income, on a mortgage that becomes an extreme burden in every sense, creating significant stress on you and your family. By addressing an Esteem need (keeping up with the Joneses), the decision put your Physiological needs at risk. While we don't walk around in life saying, "I think I'll address my Physiological needs today," our frame of reference for decision making does evolve. It's hard to think about dating and participating in a relationship when you are homeless and worried about where your next meal is coming from, or how you fear for your safety as you sleep in your car. Yet, if our basic Physiological and Safety needs are reasonably met, there are thoughts of finding your tribe that cares for you.

Buck understood how our hierarchy of needs does impact our accumulation of material riches. The questions that remained in Buck's mind was, "What form of logic do we use to make the decision to gather or accumulate things? How much is enough?" Together, Buck and I chose, for the purposes of establishing some examples in his American Dream plan, that he'd focus on the most common material items: shelter, transportation, basic household furnishings. To fuel Buck's American Dream plan, together we walked through the following questions and worksheets:

Part I: Given your current circumstances, capture
the status of these material items

Shelter	Live w/ Parents	Rent Apartment	Rent Home	Mortgaged Home	Own Home	House for Life
Transportation	Mass Transit	Share Family Car	Own Beater	Used Car Financed	New Car Financed	Own New Car
Bedroom Suite	Parent's Furniture	Curb Side Special	Used-a-Bit	Rent-to-Own New	Own — Modest	Own Dream Set
Livingroom Suite	Parent's Furniture	Curb Side Special	Used-a-Bit	Rent-to-Own New	Own — Modest	Own Dream Set
Dining Suite	Parent's Furniture	Curb Side Special	Used-a-Bit	Rent-to-Own New	Own — Modest	Own Dream Set
Laundry	Parent's	Laundry-Mat	Used-a-Bit	Rent-to-Own New	Own — Modest	Own Dream Set
Electronics: iPhone	Parent's Pkg	Pre-Paid	Older Model	Financed — Newer	Own - Newer	
TV	Parent's/ None	Used	New — Modest - Financed	New — Modest — Own	New — Beasty — Financed	New — Beasty - Own
Tablet/PC	Parent's/ None	Older Model	Financed — Newer	Own - Newer		
Gamebox	Parent's/ None	Older Model	Financed — Newer	Own - Newer		

Part II: Using the various classifications used for each item above, plot out when it is most logical to acquire/upgrade the same items as above, i.e., Shelter: Mortgaged Home in 5 years, and House for Life in 10 years

	6-Months	1 Year	3 Years	5 Years	7 Years	10 Years
Shelter:						
Transportation:						
Bedroom Suite						
Livingroom Suite						
Dining Suite						
Laundry						
Electronics: iPhone						
TV						
Tablet/PC						
Gamebox						

After completing these exercises and exchanging the logic in making these decisions, Buck became aware that he was building personal criteria, or putting in context how he would address these decisions as each opportunity unfolds in the future. This is one example of how the journey is almost more important than the American Dream plan tool. With that, Buck can check off one more battle plan. OPERATION MY STUFF — is ready to go!

CHAPTER V-C
Operation Lunchbox

BUCK KNEW WITHOUT QUESTION, a key component to his dream was the choice he'd make in terms of job and career path. He didn't take this portion of his battle planning lightly. He had heard the old adage by Confucius, "Choose a job you love, and you will never work a day in your life." Buck absolutely wanted to find a career that would make him feel like he'd never have to work. To achieve this feeling, he knew his choices had to be grounded in something he was passionate about — a passion so deep he couldn't help but feel it down to his core, and never stop thinking about it.

Like many young Americans, Buck had participated in several career fairs and job workshops. Many of these events put Buck and his peers at a job fair setting with someone asking them what kind of job are you looking for. Buck conceded a person's station in life likely would determine how they'd answer. It could be, "I just want a job that pays the bills," or it could be a very specific job, or one with a specific location or benefits package.

Visiting career experts would often present their audiences with a lay of the land in terms of people choosing jobs. A common point made was how often people change jobs over the course of a lifetime. One example of information regarding changing jobs was an article titled *How many times do people change careers in their lifetime?*, which states, "A Bureau of Labor Statistics (BLS) survey of people born between 1957 and 1964 that traced their work history through to age 52 shows that people tend to change jobs fewer times as they grow older. From ages 18 to 24, they change jobs an average of 5.7 times. Between 25 and 34 years old, they change jobs an average of 2.4 times. The average goes down again to 2.9 jobs between ages 35 and 44, and then to 1.9 jobs between ages 45 and 52."[15]

Throughout Buck's life, he had seen many of his neighbors constantly changing jobs just to get a better paycheck. Obviously, they had no loyalty to their employers, and would never find a job that spoke to who they really are. Buck could not envision himself jumping from job to job — that was just not in his DNA. So, Buck's quandary was what is he passionate about?

Buck's best friend loved Legos all the while they were growing up. He loved building outrageous structures or worlds, and that led him to becoming an engineer who became renowned for specializing in refining or fixing complex problems; it was just his happy place.

Buck had also seen several acquaintances devasted by someone close to them having to endure something unimaginable, be it cancer and an early death, or some form of assault, neglect, bullying, or deprivation; and these events were so egregious the individuals involved became committed to preventing the same for others, and therefore choosing a career path to that end.

Then there were others who were content in taking on whatever careers (or jobs) were obvious choices in their neighborhood, mostly focused around the service and trades industries. Buck was confident these folks were never going to find blissfulness in what they did. He knew his battle plan had to speak to what's in his heart. He was asking himself, "What's in my heart? What are those jobs that put me in my happy place? What continues to drive my focus in a particular direction? And what are those careers that I just totally despise?"

One solution to Buck's quandary was the opportunity to try jobs out. In one of those career fairs, he had learned he could become a volunteer at the Red Cross. Being a registered volunteer, opportunity knocks, and volunteers can experience a day in the life of someone in a given career field. This opportunity reminded Buck of a friend who always wanted to be a doctor or nurse, but after volunteering in a clinic, his friend quickly realized they were afraid of the sight of blood, and even more so with the sight of internal organs. Needless to say, his friend gave up on that career choice. After much reflection, research and job shadowing, Buck recognized what could be his happy place and career path; he used the following exercise to map out his *Operation Lunchbox* battle plan.

Exercise I — Identify your general category of your dream job: _____

- This exercise needs to be a highly personalized experience; there is no one way to accomplish this task. How this is done is left to the individual, but the approach needs to be much like a science project, with research and study.
- In the end, completing this task results in the individual identifying a particular career area, i.e., medicine, music, finance, horticulture, construction, hi-tech, etc.
- **Identify your career-field of choice?**_____

Exercise II — Research your chosen career-field — identify your ultimate dream job

- Many pursue a dream job without any comprehensive knowledge of what it entails. Chase your dream job with your eyes open to the good, bad and challenges.

- The Bureau of Labor has a great reference, the *Occupational Outlook Handbook*, which characterizes each field with the following tabs of descriptive data: Summary; What they do; Work environment; How to become one; Pay; Job outlook; State & area data; and Similar occupations.
- Use this reference to explore all the possibilities related to your chosen career-field. Pay particular attention to the "Important Qualities" in the "How to become one" tab.
- **Identify your be-all, ultimate Dream Job.** _____

    _____

- Recommendation: Do a sanity check — Go interview and shadow someone who is currently working in your Dream Job.

Exercise III — Layout the logical evolution and progression to your dream job

- Making it to your Dream Job normally doesn't involve going straight into it, but involves an evolution of developing proficiency and expertise. There will likely be an Entry job that evolves to higher level positions as you gain knowledge, skills, experience, and reputation.
- Using the following matrix, outline the normal progression path to your Dream Job. In Buck's case, his family had three generations of success in the construction industry. He was able to pick the brains of his dad and grandpa on the good, the bad, and the ugly parts of being in a trade for life. He also used information in the *Occupational Outlook Handbook* to frame his worksheet.

Job	Years of Experience	Education	License or Certifications	Other
Plumber-Helper	None	High School or GED	None	
Apprentice Plumber	None	Pre-apprenticeship Program	None	2,000 hours of paid on-the-job training/Yr
Journeyman Plumber	3-5 Years	Apprenticeship	State License	
Master Plumber	Several	Continuing Education	2nd State License	Multiple Certifications

Buck had finally chosen a dream job and knew what it was going to take to get it. OPERATION LUNCHBOX, done! By now, Buck was really seeing the landscape of his American Dream coming more and more into focus.

CHAPTER V-D
Operation DIY

NOW THAT BUCK HAD CHOSEN A CAREER PATH, he faced finding a path in terms of training and education to bring it about. He and his family were by no means wealthy. He had to find the means to make his dream a reality; it was definitely a Do It Yourself (DIY) project of significant magnitude.

What had partly contributed to Buck's career choice was the knowledge that education opens the door to a limitless American Dream. For me, Buck's acknowledgment here speaks to my mantra — if you're not changing, you're dying. Education induces change.

"A good educational system is essential for shaping the future of society. It's a fundamental part of our lives. Without education, no matter how big or small, people wouldn't be able to grow and become the best versions of themselves. Education allows us to gain more information, which helps us make better personal and business decisions.

It expands our world and allows us to develop and express our thoughts. A good educational system shapes a child into a fully functioning adult, armed with the knowledge gained during their years in school. The world becomes their oyster, and what they want to do with it is up to them. Without education, a person doesn't develop a sufficient self-dependency or sense of self. Without education, individuals would end up missing out on far more than knowledge."[16]

Buck recognized knowledge is power; knowledge was going to be his gateway to better jobs, better pay, a better life. He was feeling even more validated when he ran across these reports on average annual income by education levels from the 2020 Bureau of Labor Statistics:

Less than a high school diploma — $30,784
High school education — $38,792
Attended some college — $43,316
Two-year college degree — $46,124
Bachelor's degree — $64,896
Master's degree — $77,844
Doctorate degree — $97,916[17]

According to ZipRecruiter's *How much does a Trade make?*, "As of Jan 15, 2022, the average annual pay for a Trade in the United States is $57,204 a year."[18] Using a simple salary calculator, that works out to be approximately $27.50 an hour. This is the equivalent of $1,100/week or $4,767/month. While ZipRecruiter is seeing annual salaries as high as $119,500 and as low as $20,500, the majority of Trade salaries currently range between $36,500 (25th percentile) to $67,500 (75th percentile) with top earners (90th percentile) making $98,500 annually across the United States. The average pay range for a Trade varies greatly (by as much as $31,000), which suggests there may be many opportunities for advancement and increased pay based on skill level, location and years of experience."

In our exchanges, I reiterated getting knowledge, whether through a classroom or a job site, is very empowering and should not be discounted.

The more I know, the more I learn how
little I know. —Justin Herbert

Buck agreed, and wasn't taking the need for education lightly. He deduced the impact of education on obtaining the American Dream comes down to how well you harness and enable it, meaning it impacts every facet of life, be-it job opportunities, management of personal affairs, family wellness, interactions within societal circles, values, etc. Knowledge helps you become more aware of your inner self.

Not unlike many young Americans, knowing the importance of education was not Buck's struggle; it was finding the financial means to get it. Obviously, college and trade schools were the most common sources for Buck's education; they also can come at many levels of cost. According to CollegeData.com, "For the 2020-2021 academic year, the average price of tuition and fees came to: $37,650 at private colleges. $10,560 at public colleges (in-state residents) $27,020 at public colleges (out-of-state residents)"[19]

Given that Buck was focused on becoming a plumber, he was more interested in the education paths for the trades. Buck found an article titled *How Much Does Trade School Cost? Here's What You Need to Know,* that was right on target. According to this article, "The cost of trade school varies. Average tuition fees range from about $3,600 to $14,500 per year, but there are wide variations depending on the type of institution you attend and the program you choose. Trade schools (which are also sometimes known as technical institutes, vocational schools, or career colleges) can be either public or private, and their programs can be as short as a few months or as long as two years or more."[20]

Learning about these costs only made Buck's dilemma seem even more monumental. Covering the cost of getting educated or trained was going to be significant to making his career leap; it stirred up so many immediate thoughts, e.g., "I can't afford to go to these schools without a scholarship and scholarships are only for those with a super GPA, and that's not me." He even momentarily contemplated giving up on his career choice and doing something else. Sitting around a fire ring in my back yard Buck shared his research and conclusions with me. Fortunately, I was able to talk Buck off his momentary doom and gloom ledge by offering several alternatives.

One of them was having him review the web page for *Don't Write Off Smaller Scholarships*, which states, "While far from full rides, smaller scholarships from local organizations, professional societies, and other groups can be useful. Typically, in the range of $50 to $500, they could cover a semester's worth of textbooks or lab fees. Many times, a smaller scholarship will have fewer requirements and be less competitive. Also, these smaller scholarships are usually paid directly to the student rather than the school itself, which makes it possible to use them for a wider range of costs."[21]

- There are thousands of scholarships out there. On average applying for these scholarships require as little as an hour of effort, an application and essay on your aspirations. So, are you willing to work for $500/hour? Each of these $500 opportunities add up and can add up to a fully paid for education. Oh, by the way, there are scholarships for trade schools too!

- Scholarships are not just for students graduating from high school. There are many organizations that offer scholarships for older adults wanting to continue their education or undergo a change in careers.

- It's cheaper for companies to grow their own rather than recruiting new employees from outside their companies? So, there are many employers who offer tuition assistance or scholarships for their up-and-coming employees.

- While the military may not be for everyone, most states have the National Guard, offering signing bonuses and tuition assistance programs, with each branch of service having an abundance of jobs and technical training opportunities.

- Job impacting knowledge can also come from experiences garnered in other activities, such as work or projects you get involved in with volunteer organizations, e.g., church, community service organizations like the Red Cross, VFW, Lions Clubs, Rotary, Habitat for Humanity, etc.
- In this day and age, knowledge can be found online too, such as audio books, blogs, pod casts, video games, etc.
- There are also numerous mentorship programs out there to be had by the willing.

> My mission in life is not merely to survive, but to thrive;
> and to do so with some passion, some compassion,
> some humor, and some style. —Maya Angelou

As I kicked the ambers around in the fire ring and got the flames to reconstitute, I recalled and shared with Buck this quote from Maya Angelou that had frequently reenergized me in the past. I went onto say, "Each of us are challenged to become better informed, to make better choices. The choice remains, what can I learn to have the better jobs, better pay, better life? Each of us have the power, Buck you have the power! We can't address the solution until we know the problem. So, what specifically do you think is the missing link to finding this part of your American Dream?" He responded he still wasn't clear how he was going to become the successful plumber he could celebrate long into his retirement phase of life. We agreed to have a breakfast meeting in a few days, and to dissect the knowledge, skills and experience he would need.

Days later, in the corner booth of my favorite diner, we dug through the bits and pieces of information Buck had gathered so far. We needed to identify the logical path of progressing to Buck's Dream Job. A key part of that path was itemizing the Knowledge, Skills, and Experience required for that Dream Job and putting them into a timeline. We used the following matrix to layout when Buck was likely to achieve these milestones. To keep our focus on the somewhat-near-term, we limited our efforts to those milestones that would likely occur over the next 10 years.

Job	Knowledge, Skills and Experience	When	Source
Plumber-Helper	High School or GED	2022	Local High School
Apprentice Plumber	Pre-apprenticeship School	2022 - 2023	Local Plumbers Union School
	2,000 Hrs OJT/Yr	2022 - 2025	Jobs w/Local Contractors
	Apprentice Test	2025	State Test Site
Journeyman Plumber	3-5 Years of Proficiency	2025 - 2030	Jobs w/Local Contractors
	State License	2029 - 2030	State Test Site
Master Plumber	5-7 Years of Proficiency	2030 - 2035	Multiple Certifications
	Continuing Education	Annually	Trade/State Sponsored
	2nd State License	2035	State Test Site

Buck was able to look at this simple worksheet and see the foreseeable problems or milestones he needed to address. Since they were in bite size pieces, the problems set both in the short and long term seemed far more manageable and achievable. He was now far better postured to formulate specific strategies and alternatives to address those milestones that were most immediate. The primary objective of OPERATION DIY had been achieved. Buck was able to check one more battle plan off, and realized he only had two more to go. He had another "Wow!" moment filled with excitement.

Operation Squeeze Me

GIVEN ALL THAT BUCK HAD BEEN THROUGH growing up, he knew very well you can't walk this Earth through life without relationships, be it family loved ones, friends, associates, or a soulmate. He concluded anyone who walks through life alone will do so as a very unhappy person. Once again, sitting on the back deck, watching the sunset, Buck shared his understanding and need for relationships. Together, we accepted finding blissful happiness requires feeling good about yourself, and the directions or decisions you choose in life. To do without other people in our lives is nearly impossible. To do so, we foster a very myopic or singular perspective of life, what is good, bad, or indifferent. More importantly, because our aspirations are an ever-evolving, continuously moving target, they call for a greater understanding of life's truths and a need to continuously evolve with them; and that cannot be done without others in your life.

We reminded ourselves that historically, the American Dream is grounded in doing better than our parents, achieving multiple successes in life, sharing it all with someone special, and propelling the next generation into a new legacy. Buck was confident someday he would find the right someone and he wasn't really worried about this facet of his life; it would happen when it happened. Feeling perplexed, he didn't understand exactly why we should spend so much effort on this battle plan area. I assured him that manifesting his American Dream requires a certain degree of affirmation; reassuring himself he's making headway, it's valued, he's on the right track, and a nudge to keep it up. Most importantly, those around you have a direct impact on your American Dream, and that impact needs to be positive. For that reason, it is important for each of us to find our tribe. Sorry, my infatuation with the pioneers and Native Americans, I couldn't help but use the term "tribe" to help get my point across.

According to Oxford Languages, the term "tribe" is defined as "a social division in a traditional society consisting of families or communities linked by social, economic, religious, or blood ties, with a common culture and dialect, typically having a recognized leader."[22] Merriam-Webster.com defines a tribe as "a social group composed chiefly of numerous families, clans, or generations having a shared ancestry and language; a group of persons having a common character, occupation, or interest."[23]

We discussed how Buck's definition of his tribe would most likely start with his immediate family; it would also include his immediate group of friends and local community. His American Dream dictated the values of his tribe had to be congruent with his aspirations, and not a negative force or influence, i.e., if his tribe included a local street gang in the inner city, it was not likely going to be a positive influence. Digging deeper and through extensive reflection, we shared thoughts on other truths: as we mature, we tend to respect our family and where they came from and what they stood for; Mom or Dad will always be Mom or Dad. Hopefully, we also try to shape our adult circle of friends and acquaintances so they will have a positive impact on our life, livelihood, and success.

On Buck's journey, he'd likely sculpt a new world of friends and acquaintances, both knowingly and unknowingly. His American Dream dictated the musts and must not, i.e., if you're becoming a doctor, you are less likely to hang around a high school buddy who sells drugs on the corner, but you would hang with fellow medical professionals, or remain acquainted with college buddies. We found agreement in the notion some of our tribe members could be a distraction to our game plan. If we are to be successful, we are obliged to weigh the risks such affiliations pose and take action to minimize, if not eliminate those risks. Buck had to be the final judge, but also had to go into that judgment with his eyes wide open.

We furthered this dialog by acknowledging a more obvious and key facet of belonging was affection. Yes, our family and friends are a great source of affection; there's nothing like a hug from Mom, but it's a type of affection that is guarded on the edges, i.e., Mom doesn't know all of your inner secrets. Human nature is to want a companion that will know every facet of you, the private side that includes those personal nuances, guarded secrets, and deep-down passions that make you unique. They are the Yin to your Yang; and in all likelihood, the one you will make the next generation or version of you with.

There is a time and place where some of these relationships are a natural occurrence, and as for the others, we can curb or control when or how far those windows are open. Buck accepted these truths, but wasn't sure on how to go about planning for them. For this reason, Buck concluded this portion of his planning efforts just needed to be focused on being aware of the relationships that exist in his life and anticipating when or if he would be open to new ones. To articulate this aspect of Buck's OPERATION SQUEEZE ME, he kept it simple. He limited his thoughts to making an assessment of what his aspirations were, what it's going to take to achieve them in terms of each planning element, and asking himself what level of personal relationship would have the most positive impact on these planned events or milestones? He used these stages of personal relationships, (Single with core friends, Casual dating, Nurturing an early-on relationship, Serious long-term relationship, Married, Married with kids) and plugged them into a timeline similar to this when he felt would be most appropriate and supportive of his American Dream:

Current	
1-Year	
3-Years	
5-Years	
7-Years	
10-Years	

Once again, Buck was enjoying a moment of accomplishment. Not only had he completed another battle plan, he was on the brink of tackling his final battle plan in this journey of defining who he was to be.

CHAPTER V-F
Operation Care-Bear

BUCK'S FAMILY ENCOURAGED HIM TO HAVE FAITH. They wanted him to concentrate on becoming more self-aware by finding a spirituality that would help him find solace in practicing life truths. I was in agreement with Buck's parents. On the surface, Buck may have perceived this as a mandate of sorts, that we all need to believe in a God, and we all must have, and practice, some sort of religious faith. While Buck may have had his own personal beliefs, this segment was about a much more composite view of his station and contribution within mankind. I assured Buck there are many definitions of faith to be accounted for. Faith definition: "complete trust or confidence in someone or something; strong belief in God or in the doctrines of a religion, based on spiritual apprehension rather than proof," or "confidence or trust in a person or thing: faith in another's ability; belief that is not based on proof: He had faith that the hypothesis would be substantiated by fact; belief in God or in the doctrines or teachings of religion: the firm faith of the Pilgrims; belief in anything, as a code of ethics, standards of merit, etc.: to be of the same faith with someone concerning honesty; a system of religious belief:

the Christian faith; the Jewish faith; the obligation of loyalty or fidelity to a person, promise, engagement, etc."

I asked Buck to think back to that man who was always helping kids in the neighborhood. He asked what that man had to do with spirituality or finding solace in practicing life truths? Together, we talked through the impact the man was making. We concluded whether you are a receiver or giver, the exchange of gifts defines who you are, reminding us that we don't walk this life alone, defining how richness can be found in the simplest things in life, and portraying how those moments of richness can have a life-changing effect on both the receiver and giver. This exchange of gifts speaks to how a man walks amongst us with values that evolve into a legacy not defined by him, but by his fellow mankind. It's about personal growth, and the meaning of paying it forward. Buck had never heard the phrase "paying it forward," or at least hadn't paid attention to it when he did hear it. "Pay it forward is an expression for when the recipient of an act of kindness does something kind for someone else rather than simply accepting or repaying the original good deed."[24]

I summed up the spiritual lesson to Buck this way: on your journey toward the American Dream, if you are to be truly successful and fully appreciate the depth and scope of that achievement, you will realize the success is not just yours. Success is shared in some form or another with those you touched along the way. Otherwise, you would be like a king in an empty castle with no kingdom, or a quarterback without a team. So, I asked Buck, "What will be your legacy? Who will you bring along?"

I've always said, "People don't care how much you know, until they know how much you care." In this situation, how much you know about your fellow mankind, and your gift giving with them, are directly tied to the American Dream. OPERATION CARE-BEAR is all about defining your legacy through outward actions, demonstrating how you care about those you interact with, finding richness in giving, and finding and being guided by life's truths. Buck asked, "How do you do that?" My answer, in short, was, "Each of us will find it in our own way." Being the old guy in these efforts, I offered several thoughts about life's truths, and hoped Buck would garner a deeper understanding and appreciation for the task at hand.

As we transition between the stages of life, we have many opportunities to give. Yes, you can become involved in faith-based religious activities. You could also find yourself involved in an endless list of community-based service organizations. There are also various professional organizations that cater to your career-fields. Lastly, you might have a special interest pet project that is near and dear to your heart, i.e., curing childhood cancer. Each of these opportunities will challenge you to commit your time, labor, and means (resources). Your ability and willingness to pay it forward is something you'll likely have to nurture. As a young aspiring adult, you may not have a lot of time or resources, and you may only dabble in these types of activities. However, as you mature professionally, financially, spiritually, your ability to give back will likely grow. Eventually, you may become more and more inspired and become a leader in these endeavors.

Before Buck asked himself to identify where he'd likely pay it forward, he thought back to the 100-year celebration of life and the legacy he presumably would create. He also thought back to my stories about my favorite grandma, her house with all of those tokens of gratification from those she had helped over the years; and then my mother's commitment to family and all those Christmas holidays made special, even in the worst of times. Those stories and similar ones from his own family history were inspirational to Buck. He knew those values were an integral part of who he is. He thought paying it forward would very much be part of his legacy.

With his battle planning efforts coming to an end, Buck took the opportunity to carve special stops into his journey where he thought he'd be ready and able to do his part and pay it forward. We used the following exercise to capture Buck's thoughts on opportunities to pay it forward:

Exercise

This is your opportunity to carve into your schedule what you foresee as the manner in which you will pay it forward; and how you will nurture it over your lifetime. Remember, life requires constant growth; again, if you are not changing, you are dying. From the sample activities and roles listed below, plot out how you currently envision how you'll pay it forward over the course of your life:

- **Sample Activities**: Faith-based, Community Service, Professional Organization, Fraternal Organization, Pet Project, Civic
- **Sample Roles:** Participant, Volunteer, Leader, Project Coordinator, Organizer, Teacher

	Activity	Role
Current		
1-Year		
3-Years		
5-Years		
7-Years		
10-Years		

Using this very simple approach, Buck was able to capture what was near and dear to his heart and itemize what and when he envisioned would be his opportunities to give back. As I reviewed his work and heard his reasons for including each input, I could feel his passion coming to the forefront. Buck was also feeling a deep sense of accomplishment when he realized he had finished his final battle plan. OPERATION CARE-BEAR was done! He was just overwhelmingly jubilant!

CHAPTER VI
A Map Like No Other

NOW IT WAS TIME FOR BUCK to really appreciate the work he had completed. He also had to know work remains to bring it all together into a meaningful form that has everyday utility; the 1-page dream plan. As a matter of summarizing Buck's efforts, I sat down with him, asked him to walk me through the information he had gathered for each of his battle plans. We took each plan, one-by-one, and summarized his thoughts and conclusions.

- Operation Bank: That (Financial independence)
- Operation My Stuff: (Accumulation of Material Belongings)
- Operation DIY: (Education — Tooling a path)
- Operation Lunchbox: (Building a Career — Employment)
- Operation Squeeze Me: (Bonds of Relationship — shared)
- Operation Care-Bear: (Spiritually — Solace in practicing life truths)

As Buck spoke to each battle plan, he broke out the supporting worksheets of information. While we reviewed each plan, we gave each its own place on the kitchen table; in the end, the entire table was covered. I applauded Buck for working so hard, and told him to pat himself on the back! I asked, "Who else do you know that would work this hard on a plan for life?" We went on to discuss his journey up to this point, and the lessons he learned about himself and the man he wants to be. As Buck expressed himself, I could see a level of maturity far above his peers. We had started with a block-shaped stone and kept chipping away at it to reveal a dream that only Buck could see and find.

Rhetorically, I asked, "What was your purpose, mission, or motivation for doing all this work?" I reminded him when we started this process, his mission was to achieve a lifelong happiness, tailor-made just for him. I asked Buck if he could imagine how best he'll use this information on a daily basis and in his decision making? How often will he reference it? In its current form, how easy will it be to reference it? How are you going to keep the integrity of each plan while simultaneously working on the others?

I responded that to be fully successful, he was at a point where he needed to synchronize all those battle plans into one cohesive, comprehensive war plan, that will foster self-control across each endeavor. This step is all about drawing a map or creating a dashboard compass that will guide you throughout your life's journey for years to come...hopefully, to see that 100-year celebration you've so often envisioned. We stacked up the battle plans into a neat pile and replaced our focus on a blank 1-page American

Dream Plan. From there, we walked step-by- step to pull information from the pile of battle plans and migrate it all onto the 1-page document. We used the following steps:

My American Dream Road Map As of date: _____

	Currently	Less Than 1 Year	1 – 3 Years	3 – 5 Years	5 Years	American Dream End-Sate
Materially						
Financially						
Employment						
Education						
Family						
Spiritually						

Step 1: Column 1 (Currently):

Using the data you previously gathered, populate each row (Category) with a narrative description of your current circumstances.

I noted to Buck, while we could probably write a novel in each block, we want this to be easily readable at a glance, like mile markers on the highway. So, we should highlight the big nuggets, limiting the descriptors in each block to 3 to 4 short bullet-type phrases, i.e., Age-20, $15K in debt, High School Grad, Plumber's Helper, applying for Plumber's Apprenticeship Program, Live with Parents, Single, Own used car, etc.

Step 2: Column 6 (American Dream — End State):

Using the data you previously gathered, populate each row (category) with a narrative description of what your American Dream state will look like.

Example of descriptors: Own my dream house, have latest technology gadgets, be living debt free, travel abroad annually, be a millionaire, retired contractor @ 50 years old, licensed master plumber, married with 3 kids & 10 grandkids, church leader, leading mentorship program, etc.

Step 3: Column 2 (Less than 1 Year):

Using the data you previously gathered, populate each row (category) with a narrative description of what changes or progress you can make in less than 1 year.

Examples of descriptors: Age-21, $7K in debt, living by a strict budget, have $1K emergency fund, enrolled in Plumber's Apprenticeship Program, working as Plumber's apprentice, continue to live with parents, single, own used car, etc.

Step 4: Column 3 (1 - 3 Years):

Using the data you previously gathered, populate each row (category) with a narrative description of what changes or progress you can make in a time frame of 1 to 3 years.

Examples of descriptors: Age-23, zero debt, living by a strict budget, have emergency fund equal to 6 months of expenses ($10K), saving for a new car ($15K), completed Plumber's Apprenticeship Program, working as Plumber's apprentice, transitioning to journeyman jobs, Union member, live in an apartment, minimal/basic furnishings, Single w/casual dating, Own same used car, volunteer at community center, etc.

Step 5: Column 4 (3 — 5 Years):

Using the data you previously gathered, populate each row (Category) with a narrative description of what changes or progress you can make between year 3 and year 5.

Examples of descriptors: Age-25, Zero debt, living by a strict budget, have emergency fund equal 6 months of expenses ($15K), saving for first house ($50K), became licensed journeyman, studying for welding certifications, working as journeyman, union member, live in an apartment, minimal/basic furnishings, single w/someone special, still have newer car, on local softball team at community center, etc.

Step 6: Column 5 (5 Years):

Using the data you previously gathered, populate each row (category) with a narrative description of what changes or progress you can make in year 5 or later.

Examples of descriptors: Age-25+, zero debt, living by a strict budget, have emergency fund equal to 6 months of expenses ($20K), Mortgaged (15 year) entry level house, minimal/basic furnishings, licensed journeyman w/welding certification, working as journeyman, union member, single w/ someone special, still have newer car, on local softball team, coaching little league at community center, etc.

Using the information provided above Buck's road map looked like this:

My American Dream Road Map As of date: _____

	Currently	Less Than 1 Year	1 – 3 Years	3 – 5 Years	5 Years	American Dream End-Sate
Materially	Live with Parents Own used car	Continue to live with Parents Own used car	Live in an apartment Minimal/basic furnishings Own same used car	Live in an apartment Minimal/basic furnishings Have newer car	Entry level house, Minimal/basic furnishings Still have newer car	Own my dream house Have latest technology gadgets
Financially	$15K in debt	$7K in debt Living by a strict budget Have $1K emergency fund	Zero debt Living by a strict budget Have 6 month emergency fund ($10K), Saving for new car ($15K)	Zero debt Living by a strict budget Have 6 months of emergency fund ($15K), Saving for first house ($50K)	Mortgaged (15 Yr) Zero debt otherwise Living by a strict budget Have 6 month emergency fund ($20K)	Living debt free Millionaire Retired @ 50 yrs old
Employment	Plumber's Helper	Working as Plumber's apprentice	Working as Plumber's apprentice, Transitioning to journeyman jobs Union member	Working as journeyman Union member	Working as journeyman Union member	Licensed master plumber Contractor
Education	High School Grad Applying for Plumber's Apprenticeship Program	Enrolled in Plumber's Apprenticeship Program	Completed Plumber's Apprenticeship Program	Became licensed Journeyman Studying for welding certifications	Licensed Journeyman w/welding certification	
Family	Age-20 Single	Age-21 Single	Age-23 Single w/casual dating	Age-25 Single w/someone special	Age-25+ Single w/someone special	Married with 3 kids & 10 grandkids
Spiritually			Volunteer at community center	On local softball team at community center	Local softball team Coaching little league at community center	Church leader Leading mentorship program Travel abroad annually

For Buck, seeing his completed worksheet and all those battle plans, he found himself overwhelmed. Initially, Buck thought, "That's it?" He could have done this in one setting. I responded by picking at various pieces of his plan and interrogated him on the What, When, Where, and Why of each. I kept poking at his plan. He became very defensive, feeling very righteous in every one of his decisions. I followed up by asking him why he was becoming so defensive? Seeing Buck's almost hateful sneer, I could tell he was extremely agitated. He stared at the 1-page plan for the longest time, and he found himself imagining his sweat lodge experience. Over the course of the experience, he could see his life's journey coming to fruition just as he imagined, but in a choreography of minuet scenes. Buck was imagining his 100-year celebration, with all his family and friends, and the flurry of emotions that would be present. In the end, Buck responded very passionately, "This is my plan, not yours! This is my dream, not yours!" Seeing Buck's response, I knew this was far more than a 1-page sketch; he was owning, really owning, every part of it. I patted him on the back and told him, "Yes, it's your plan, your choices, your dream; I'm proud of you!"

I also assured him had he just penciled in the worksheet, without taking the journey, he would not be so passionate. His passion came from the in-depth understanding of each element he nurtured along his journey. I then asked Buck, "Is it complete? Is it ready prime time?"

CHAPTER VII
What's Next?

IN MY CONGRATULATIONS TO BUCK, I pointed out he had accomplished something that millions of people won't or don't! I asked him to think about how much time he had put into creating this tool. Based on an hourly rate, he had probably invested several hundreds, if not a thousand or more dollars' worth of time. That's nothing to sneeze at, but with that said, this 1-page is intended to be a tool to be used. Otherwise, it has no value and is wasted effort.

I prompted Buck to do one final sanity check. After getting him to reflect back to when he had created a vision board, we broke it out and studied its content. Together, we evaluated whether Buck's plan addressed the following:

- Does your American Dream Road Map capture everything you envisioned?
- Are there any notions where your roadmap would have you do something that you were passionately opposed?
- Is your roadmap realistic or achievable?

- Are there major gaps between your current circumstances and your end-state American Dream that you haven't addressed in some form?
- Is this road map meaningful to you — meaning you can really embrace it and push forward with your journey?
- Did your road map capture your passion?

Wherever Buck found a gap he went back to his individual battle plans to find solutions and adjusted his road map accordingly. Having made those final adjustments, Buck and I enjoyed a celebratory BBQ on the back deck, which gave us a chance to discuss what's next. He was filled with exuberance as he talked about his dream. Truthfully, I couldn't shut him up! Buck was chomping at the bit to make it happen. Sipping a cocktail, watching massive flocks of geese flying overhead making their annual trek south, we talked about what they would likely see and experience over the 4,000 miles they would travel. We were in awe at how committed the geese had to be to getting to their southern destination. This prompted me to ask Buck about the trek ahead for him. I asked if he could imagine taking a 4K mile cross country road trip much like the geese? You would have to create a travel route, an itinerary of road stops and special interests, set a budget for spending along the way, and a list of things you wanted to experience.

With the travel plan done, there would be the moment to jump in the car and head out. To keep you on track and focused, you obviously would keep your road map handy. Knowing how zealous you tend to be, you would likely go so as far as plugging your plan into your car's GPS travel mapping system that keeps you abreast of your progress, upcoming turns, speed limits, travel warnings, points of interest, and re-routes you when a turn is missed, etc. It would be a sure-fire way to get everything you wanted out of this trip. I implored Buck to use that same zeal in using his dream plan, emphasizing it needs to be his priority. I shared this quote by Danny Griffin to solidify my point. With that understanding, I challenged Buck to make his road map as visible as possible. He should post it on his refrigerator or in some other prominent place that he'd see every day, maybe even alongside his vision board.

> My passion is my priority. I do not live my life
> chasing dreams anymore. I have commited my
> life to catching them. —Danny Griffin

I also reminded Buck that along his journey, there will be days of excitement and accomplishment, but there will also be days of questioning, discouragement, self-doubt, etc., so, he will need cheerleaders. He would need help from his circle of friends and family, wanting them to understand his American Dream and the road map he created. More importantly, he would want them to understand his level of commitment in making this dream a reality. He needed them to be supportive, and not offer him temptations that are counter to his efforts, i.e., if he's working on eliminating his debt and willing to eat beans and rice to do so, he doesn't want his friends and family to tempt him with frivolous opportunities to spend money.

Buck's road map wasn't just a post card destination! It had to be much like the dashboard instruments in his car. He'd use the dashboard to guide him throughout his journey. Along his trips, there will be hiccups, the unexpected will happen, and don't freak out when the *check engine light* or the *oil change due* indicator comes on. With his plan in hand, he will anticipate the need for preventive maintenance or unscheduled events. With this in mind, I recommended the following maintenance:

- Treat the unveiling of your American Dream Road Map as a major life-changing event, like getting married, and celebrate the anniversary every year. Use your celebration to identify and celebrate your successes, and to make any fine-tuning adjustments.

- Like wedding anniversaries, every 5 or 10 years should come with an extra special celebration. Yes, you will continue to celebrate your successes, but this will be the time when you give your road map a major update in columns 1 through 5. Don't forget to dust off those battle plans — they still have information that didn't make your previous edition of your road map.

- Revisiting your road map when there's a major life-changing event like getting married is equally important, because at that point, the road map is not just yours, it's part of your new partnership. You don't want a case of you practicing a debt free lifestyle and your partner spending uncontrollably. It will likely be very beneficial to do a joint road map so you can share in a unified dream and the journey toward it.

As Buck and I finished our cocktails on the deck and the sunset brandished a skyline of clouds with hews of pink and orange, I asked him a final question. "How do you eat an elephant? One bite at a time. Your American Dream is your elephant. The table is set. You've built a mighty war plan on how you'll attack it; now it's time to dig in. Good luck!"

The Rest of the Story

BUCK USED HIS PLAN with an unmatched vigor. He was compulsive! He ate that elephant, all of it!

He made the annual review a celebration over dinner with family and friends.

He shared with them his accomplishments, as well as his short comings.

He spoke about major changes in his life and updates to his plan.

He thanked them for their continued support.

Buck had found bliss, a heart-warming, peaceful bliss in life. He found his happiness - that was readily apparent and visible when others were in his presence — his face glowed.

While it's just been over two decades since he started his journey, he did achieve nearly everything he originally envisioned, he never stopped refining his dream, kept moving the goal posts. He found, and experienced every day, the happiness he had wished for. He paid it forward — giving became magical; be it giving of his resources, time, or labor, it was impactful! Probably the most significant part of Buck's journey wasn't the happiness he found, but rather the pathway he exemplified for several hundreds of others, who walked the journey with him.

Asked many times about the success and the obvious contentment he achieved, Buck would advise those around him to be deliberate, driven, passionate, giving, and most importantly, to never stop evolving in who you are — it's never too late.

To this author, Buck's journey is the epitome of a young American adult accepting the American Dream is anything you want it to be, and it is possible if you have the ability, aspiration, and drive to achieve it; and willfully pursue a state of happiness defined only by you, within the liberty afforded you.

Declaration of Independence

In Congress, July 4, 1776

THE UNANIMOUS DECLARATION of the thirteen united States of **America,** When in the Course of human events, it becomes necessary for one people to dissolve the political bands which have connected them with another, and to assume among the powers of the earth, the separate and equal station to which the Laws of Nature and of Nature›s God entitle them, a decent respect to the opinions of mankind requires that they should declare the causes which impel them to the separation.

We hold these truths to be self-evident, that all men are created equal, that they are endowed by their Creator with certain unalienable Rights, that among these are Life, Liberty and the pursuit of Happiness.—*That to secure these rights, Governments are instituted among Men, deriving their just powers from the consent of the governed,* —*That whenever any Form of Government becomes destructive of these ends, it is the Right of the People to alter or to abolish it, and to institute new Government, laying its foundation* *on such principles and organizing its powers in such form, as to them shall seem most likely to effect their Safety and Happiness. Prudence, indeed, will dictate that Governments long established should not be changed for light and transient causes; and accordingly all experience hath shewn, that mankind are more disposed to suffer, while evils are sufferable, than to right themselves by abolishing the forms to which they are accustomed. But when a long train of abuses and usurpations, pursuing invariably the same Object evinces a design to reduce them under absolute Despotism, it is their right, it is their duty, to throw off such Government, and to provide new Guards for their future security.--Such has been the patient sufferance of these Colonies; and such is now the necessity which constrains them to alter their former Systems of Government. The history of the present King of Great Britain is a history of repeated injuries and usurpations, all having in direct object the establishment of an absolute Tyranny over these States. To prove this, let Facts be submitted to a candid world.*

He has refused his Assent to Laws, the most wholesome and necessary for the public good.

He has forbidden his Governors to pass Laws of immediate and pressing importance, unless suspended in their operation till his Assent should be obtained; and when so suspended, he has utterly neglected to attend to them.

He has refused to pass other Laws for the accommodation of large districts of people, unless those people would relinquish the right of Representation in the Legislature, a right inestimable to them and formidable to tyrants only.

He has called together legislative bodies at places unusual, uncomfortable, and distant from the depository of their public Records, for the sole purpose of fatiguing them into compliance with his measures.

He has dissolved Representative Houses repeatedly, for opposing with manly firmness his invasions on the rights of the people.

He has refused for a long time, after such dissolutions, to cause others to be elected; whereby the Legislative powers, incapable of Annihilation, have returned to the People at large for their exercise; the State remaining in the mean time exposed to all the dangers of invasion from without, and convulsions within.

He has endeavoured to prevent the population of these States; for that purpose obstructing the Laws for Naturalization of Foreigners; refusing to pass others to encourage their migrations hither, and raising the conditions of new Appropriations of Lands.

He has obstructed the Administration of Justice, by refusing his Assent to Laws for establishing Judiciary powers.

He has made Judges dependent on his Will alone, for the tenure of their offices, and the amount and payment of their salaries.

He has erected a multitude of New Offices, and sent hither swarms of Officers to harrass our people, and eat out their substance.

He has kept among us, in times of peace, Standing Armies without the Consent of our legislatures.

He has affected to render the Military independent of and superior to the Civil power.

He has combined with others to subject us to a jurisdiction foreign to our constitution, and unacknowledged by our laws; giving his Assent to their Acts of pretended Legislation:

For Quartering large bodies of armed troops among us:

For protecting them, by a mock Trial, from punishment for any Murders which they should commit on the Inhabitants of these States:

For cutting off our Trade with all parts of the world:

For imposing Taxes on us without our Consent:

For depriving us in many cases, of the benefits of Trial by Jury:

For transporting us beyond Seas to be tried for pretended offences

For abolishing the free System of English Laws in a neighbouring Province, establishing therein an Arbitrary government, and enlarging its Boundaries so as to render it at once an example and fit instrument for introducing the same absolute rule into these Colonies:

For taking away our Charters, abolishing our most valuable Laws, and altering fundamentally the Forms of our Governments:

For suspending our own Legislatures, and declaring themselves invested with power to legislate for us in all cases whatsoever.

He has abdicated Government here, by declaring us out of his Protection and waging War against us.

He has plundered our seas, ravaged our Coasts, burnt our towns, and destroyed the lives of our people.

He is at this time transporting large Armies of foreign Mercenaries to compleat the works of death, desolation and tyranny, already begun with circumstances of Cruelty & perfidy scarcely paralleled in the most barbarous ages, and totally unworthy the Head of a civilized nation.

He has constrained our fellow Citizens taken Captive on the high Seas to bear Arms against their Country, to become the executioners of their friends and Brethren, or to fall themselves by their Hands.

He has excited domestic insurrections amongst us, and has endeavoured to bring on the inhabitants of our frontiers, the merciless Indian Savages, whose known rule of warfare, is an undistinguished destruction of all ages, sexes and conditions.

In every stage of these Oppressions We have Petitioned for Redress in the most humble terms: Our repeated Petitions have been answered only by repeated injury. A Prince whose character is thus marked by every act which may define a Tyrant, is unfit to be the ruler of a free people.

Nor have We been wanting in attentions to our Brittish brethren. We have warned them from time to time of attempts by their legislature to extend an unwarrantable jurisdiction over us. We have reminded them of the circumstances of our emigration and settlement here. We have appealed to their native justice and magnanimity, and we have conjured them by the ties of our common kindred to disavow these usurpations, which, would inevitably interrupt our connections and correspondence. They too have been deaf to the voice of justice and of consanguinity. We must, therefore, acquiesce in the necessity, which denounces our Separation, and hold them, as we hold the rest of mankind, Enemies in War, in Peace Friends.

We, therefore, the Representatives of the united States of America, in General Congress, Assembled, appealing to the Supreme Judge of the world for the rectitude of our intentions, do, in the Name, and by Authority of the good People of these Colonies, solemnly publish and declare, That these United Colonies are, and of Right ought to be Free and Independent States; that they are Absolved from all Allegiance to the British Crown, and that all political connection between them and the State of Great Britain, is and ought to be totally dissolved; and that as Free and Independent States, they have full Power to levy War, conclude Peace, contract Alliances, establish Commerce, and to do all other Acts and Things which Independent States may of right do. And for the support of this Declaration, with a firm reliance on the protection of divine Providence, we mutually pledge to each other our Lives, our Fortunes and our sacred Honor.

About the Author

HOWARD RIXIE is one of eight children, born and raised in Illinois and has resided in Alaska for the past forty years. Having served the Air Force for forty-two years, he is a decorated go-to expert in Human Resource Management, Training Development, Total Quality Management, and Industrial Engineering spectrums.

Owner/Consultant of Quality Inventing Futures, for more than 25 years. A Specialist in assisting failing small businesses, business start-ups, and training development, with an innate gift for strategic planning, process management, instructional systems design, and team building.

Howard is committed to paying it forward through community service. He embodies "If you aren't changing, you are dying" with a passion for mentoring young adults in life choices.

Howard coaches young adults looking to achieve the true American dream. To work with Howard, email: hsrixie@gmail.com.

American Dream Mentoring

HOWARD RIXIE'S AMERICAN DREAM MENTORING inspires journeys that change generations to come!

Howard Rixie is a tested speaker, life coach and entrepreneur committed to helping young adults find a path in life that changes and transforms their default career paths, livelihoods, lifestyles, and stations in life to the unimaginable.

Howard brings small groups of young adults together and coaches them through a life planning process that fosters a journey to understanding their inner self, finding real passions, and plotting a path to lifelong success, achievement and enrichment.

> **It's about** … "*a young American adult accepting the American Dream is anything you want it to be, and is possible, if you have the ability, aspiration, and drive to achieve it; and willfully pursue a state of happiness defined only by you, within the liberty afforded you.*"

Owner/Consultant of *Quality Inventing Futures,* for more than 25 years.

Numerous government, education and non-profit entities have reaped benefits from Howard's gift for strategic planning, process management, instructional systems design, survey development, and team building. Howard offers seminars on all of these subjects tailored to each client's needs.

To book a session contact

Howard Rixie at Quality Inventing Futures
Email: Hsrixie@gmail.com
Cell: (907) 378-7797
Facebook: Quality Inventing Futures
QIF-AK.com

Endnotes

1   "Sweat Lodge." n.d. Pluralism.org. https://pluralism.org/sweat-lodge.

2   "Dream Board." 2022. Wikipedia. May 9, 2022. https://en.wikipedia.org/wiki/Dream_board.

3   investopedia. 2019. "Sharper Insight. Smarter Investing." Investopedia. 2019. https://www.investopedia.com/.

4   "Dave Ramsey." n.d. Ramsey Solutions. https://www.ramseysolutions.com/dave-ramsey?snid=personalities.ramsey-personalities.dave-ramsey.

5   "A Proven Plan for Financial Success | RamseySolutions.com." n.d. Ramsey Solutions. https://www.ramseysolutions.com.

6   "EveryDollar | Make a Budget and Track Expenses." n.d. Ramsey Solutions. https://www.ramseysolutions.com/ramseyplus/everydollar.

7   "Gazelle Intensity: Do You Have It?" n.d. Ramsey Solutions. Accessed May 26, 2022. https://www.ramseysolutions.com/debt/gazelle-intensity-do-you-have-it.

8   "Welcome to CK-12 Foundation | CK-12 Foundation." n.d. Www.ck12.org. Accessed May 26, 2022. https://

www.ck12.org/user:yxblcmtpbnnaz2nib2uudxm./book/
giles-county-tennessee-fifth-grade-social-studies/section/6.2.

9   "A Consumer Economy [Ushistory.org]." 2019. Ushistory.org. 2019.
    https://www.ushistory.org/us/46f.asp.

10 "The State of Debt among Americans." n.d. Ramsey Solutions. https://www.
    ramseysolutions.com/debt/state-of-debt-among-americans-research.

11 Shrider, Emily A., Melissa Kollar, Frances Chen, and Jessica Semega.
    2021. "Income and Poverty in the United States: 2020." The United States
    Census Bureau. September 14, 2021. https://www.census.gov/library/
    publications/2021/demo/p60-273.html.

12 "The State of Debt among Americans." n.d. Ramsey Solutions. https://www.
    ramseysolutions.com/debt/state-of-debt-among-americans-research.

13 Shrider, Emily A., Melissa Kollar, Frances Chen, and Jessica Semega.
    2021. "Income and Poverty in the United States: 2020." The United States
    Census Bureau. September 14, 2021. https://www.census.gov/library/
    publications/2021/demo/p60-273.html.

14 Desmet, Pieter, and Steven Fokkinga. 2020. "Beyond Maslow's Pyramid:
    Introducing a Typology of Thirteen Fundamental Needs for Human-
    Centered Design." Multimodal Technologies and Interaction 4 (3): 38.
    https://doi.org/10.3390/mti4030038.

15 "How Often Do People Change Careers?" n.d. Indeed Career
    Guide. https://www.indeed.com/career-advice/starting-new-job/
    how-often-do-people-change-careers.

16 "College Search, Financial Aid, College Application, College Scholarship,
    Student Loan, FAFSA, Common Application." n.d. CollegeData. https://
    www.collegedata.com

17 Torpey, Elka. 2021. "Education Pays, 2020 Career Outlook: U.S. Bureau
    of Labor Statistics." Www.bls.gov. June 2021. https://www.bls.gov/career-
    outlook/2021/data-on-display/education-pays.htm.

18 "Trade Annual Salary ($57,204 Avg | Nov 2020)." n.d. ZipRecruiter.
    https://www.ziprecruiter.com/Salaries/Trade-Salary.

19 "How Much Does College Cost?" 2020. CollegeData. 2020. https://www.collegedata.com/resources/pay-your-way/whats-the-price-tag-for-a-college-education.

20 "How Much Does Trade School Cost." n.d. Www.schools-Education.com. Accessed May 26, 2022. https://www.schools-education.com/how-much-does-trade-school-cost/.

21 "How Much Can a Student Win from Scholarships?" 2019. Investopedia. 2019. https://www.investopedia.com/articles/personal-finance/121015/how-much-can-students-realistically-get-scholarships.asp.

22 Oxford Languages. 2022. "Oxford Languages and Google - English." Languages.oup.com. Oxford University Press. 2022. https://languages.oup.com/google-dictionary-en/

23 https://www.merriam-webster.com/

24 Dictionary.com. 1995. "Dictionary.com - the World's Favorite Online Dictionary!" Dictionary.com. Dictionary.com. 1995. https://www.dictionary.com/.

Made in the USA
Middletown, DE
14 March 2025